The Costa Rica Puzzle Book

MW00928166

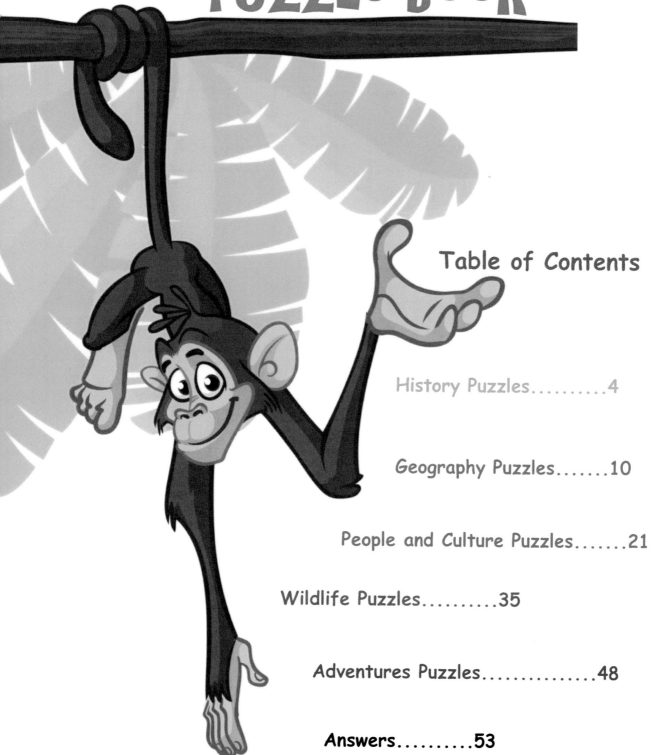

Table of Contents

Jack L. Roberts

Michael Owens

Credits

Publisher: Curious Kids Press, Palm Springs, CA 92264.
Designed by: Michael Owens
Editor: Sterling Moss
Copy Editor: Janice Ross

Special thanks to our student puzzle testers: Jason Waterson, 11 years old and Angelina Garcia-Diaz, 10 years old.

Curious Kids Press books are available at special discount when purchased in bulk for premiums, sales promotions, or educational fund-raising activities. In addition, we also create special sponsored editions, designed to meet marketing and/or promotional objectives of our clients. To learn more about our customized editions, contact Jack Roberts, publisher, at info@curiouskidspress.com

Copyright © 2018 by Curious Kids Press. All rights reserved. Except that any text portion of this book may be reproduced – mechanically, electronically, by hand or any other means you can think of – by any kid, anywhere, any time. For more information: info@curiouskidspress.com or 760-992-5962.
Printed in the United States of America.

About This Book

WHAT'S MORE FUN than a barrel of monkeys? How about a barrel (or book) of puzzles about *Costa Rican* monkeys and everything else about this totally awesome country.

That's what you'll find in this book – more than 40 crosswords puzzles, word search puzzles, picture puzzles, mazes, and more – along with a few brain twisters thrown in.

Each puzzle has a special fun fact or coded message about Costa Rica – its history, geography, people and culture, wildlife, and, of course, the amazing adventures in this awesome country!

When working the puzzles, keep a couple of things in mind:

- **Word Search**: The words always run in a straight line in the puzzle grid. But they may run horizontally, vertically, or diagonally. They also may run forwards and backwards, and they may overlap or cross each other. For example, the last two letters in the word *wash* could start the word *shut*. Finally, remember to cross off the words in the Word List as you find them in the puzzle.

- **Rebus:** A rebus is a special kind of short puzzle made up of words and/or pictures. You really have to "think outside the box" to solve a rebus, just like the rebus below shows you:

- **Acrostic**: An acrostic is like a Crossword puzzle and an a hidden or coded message put together. Your goal is to reveal a hidden message or group of related words. Each letter in the coded message is linked to a letter in one of the clue answers. It helps to work back and forth between the Coded Message and the Clues.

- **Answers**: In case you get stumped on a puzzle (or just want to take a sneak peek at the answer), you will find all of the puzzle answers at the end of this book, beginning on page 53.

Here's hoping you have more fun than a barrel of monkeys with this puzzle book – and discover lots of fun facts about Costa Rica at the same time.

The Staff of Curious Kids Press

Costa Rica History Puzzles

Columbus "Discovers" Costa Rica

ON MAY 12, 1502, fifty-one-year-old Christopher Columbus sailed from Cádiz, Spain, on his fourth and final voyage to the New World. Four months later, on September 18, 1502, he came across land that would later be called Costa Rica.

See if you can find your way from Cadiz, Spain, to Costa Rica in this maze.

Start Your Voyage Here: Cádiz, Spain

Costa Rica

Maze: Licensed from mazegenerator.net

What Columbus Named Costa Rica

SOME PEOPLE say that Columbus gave this new land the name Costa Rica. But actually he called it something else. Find out that name in this puzzle.

The completed crossword grid (handwritten answers):

1 a	2 d	3 s			4 l	5 e	6 s	
7 c	u	t	8 s		9 a	r	k	
10 h	o	o	t		11 t	e	a	12 m
		r	13 b	e			14 t	o
15 t	16 h	e	17 g	a	r	18 d	e	n
19 h	e		20 a	t		r		
21 e	a	22 r	s		23 s	e	24 t	25 s
	26 t	o	e		27 t	a	i	l
28 s	i	s			29 m	a	y	

Across

1. Short for advertisements.
4. Short for Leslie.
7. Separates in two or more pieces.
9. Noah's _____.
10. To make a quick, short sound on a horn.
11. A group of players on one of the sides of a sporting event.
13. Shakespeare: "To _____ or not to be."
14. "Give it _____ me."
15. **NAME COLUMBUS GAVE COSTA RICA. (**two words)
19. Opposite of she.
20. Finally: _____ last.
21. What you hear with.
23. What the sun does in the evening.
26. What you might stub.
27. The long rear part of the body of some animals.
28. Short for sister.
29. Fifth month of the year.

Down

1. A major division of a play.
2. Pair of singers.
3. Place to shop for food: grocery _____.
4. "Sooner or _____."
5. Old word for *before*; sounds like "air."
6. To move or glide on ice.
8. Abbreviation for street.
12. Abbreviation for Monday.
13. _____ and ball.
15. Famous kids' book: "Charlie and _____ Chocolate Factory."
16. Warms up, such as food.
17. Fills up a car tank: _____ up.
18. What you often do when you're asleep.
22. French for king.
23. Same as 8 Down.
24. Spanish for aunt.
25. Crafty; clever: "_____ as a fox."

Rebus

Whom did Columbus meet when he arrived in present-day Costa Rica?

TribeS   Tribes   **Tribes**   Tribes

Write your answer here:

Tribes

5

What Does It Mean?

MOST HISTORIANS say that a Spanish conquistador named Gil Gonzálas Dávilla gave Costa Rica its name in 1522. But what does the name Costa Rica mean? Finish this puzzle to find out.

1 L	2 O	3 L			4 a	5 m		
6 a	r	u			7		8	9
	10 e			11		12		
		13 i	14		15		16	
17	18	n				19		
20			21					
22		23				24	25	
26		27		28			29	
	30				31			

Across

1. Laugh Out Loud, for short.
4. Opposite of PM.
6. Dry, as in a desert.
7. What to wear outside in winter.
10. Central American country: ____ Salvador.
12. What to say at a bullfight.
13. At or on the highest point; the top of.
16. What you might add at the end of a letter (abbreviated).
17. **WHAT COSTA RICA MEANS** (two words).
20. Proverb: "____ apple a day keeps the doctor away."
21. What one does at supper.
22. Saying: "Can't judge a book by _____ cover."
24. Laugh word.
26. In grammar, a word that names a person, place, or thing.
28. A microscopic organism, such as a virus, that causes illness.
30. _____, myself, and I.
31. Saying: "_____no evil; hear no evil, speak no evil."

Down

1. Los Angeles, for short.
2. A mineral or rock substance.
3. Kind of flower, often purple in color.
4. Air conditioning, for short.
5. Sound a cow makes.
8. Snowy mountain system in Europe.
9. Another word for quiz or exam.
11. Center of activity or interest: "_____ point." (Rhymes with local.)
14. Dr. Seuss book: "_____ Cat in the Hat."
15. Something to cook in.
17. Come _____or shine.
18. Opposite of out of.
19. What a burning cigarette leaves; cinders.
23. The addition of two or more numbers.
25. Song: "We ____ the World."
27. Short for Northeast.
29. Same as 30 Across.

Picture Puzzle
National Coat of Arms

A COAT OF ARMS is a painted symbol or design that represents a country. It is often painted on a shield.

Almost all countries have a coat of arms – just like they have a national flag, a national anthem, and a national day.

Take a look at the two pictures of Costa Rica's coat of arms below. The two pictures may look the same. But look again. There are ten differences in the one on the right. Can you find the differences? Circle or highlight what you find.

Fun Fact

On August 9, 1884, San Jose got something no other city in Central America had at that time. What was it? To find out, use this simple code:

1 = a 2 = b 3 = c 4 = d 5 = e 6 = f 7 = g 8 = h 9 = i 10 = j 11 = k 12 = l 13 = m

14 = n 15 = o 16 = p 17 = q 18 = r 19 = s 20 = t 21 = u 22 = v 23 = w 24 = x 25 = y 26 = z

___ ___ ___ ___ ___ ___ ___ ___ ___ ___ ___
  5   12   5   3   20   18   9   3   9   20   25

Costa Rican Holiday

ONE OF THE MOST important holidays in Costa Rica is celebrated on September 15 each year. That's the day Costa Rica gained its independence from a country in Europe. What country was it? Finish this puzzle to find out.

Across

1. Short for Leslie.
4. Adhesive: Scotch _____.
8. Swearing in: Taking the _____ of office.
10. Original thought: Bright _____.
11. What you might do at a scary movie.
13. Idiom: "_____ cool as a cucumber."
14. Something you might find at the seashore.
15. Utilize: He likes to _____ a pencil when working crossword puzzles.
16. ANSWER TO PUZZLE QUESTION.
18. What you put in a car to make it run.
20. Important religious leader and prophet mentioned many times in the Bible.
23. Army command: "_____ ease."
24. Dwarfs' marching song: Heigh-ho, heigh-ho; it's off _____ _____ we go." (two words).
25. The _____ Ranger.
27. Untruth: "That's _____ _____ ." (two words)
28. Word at the end of some prayers.
29. Water droplets that collect, usually at night, on cool lawns.

Down

1. Profit and _____.
2. Saying: "To _____ his own."
3. Mental or emotional pressure.
4. Short for Timothy.
5. Short for advertisement.
6. Idiom: "Like two _____ in a pod."
7. Not hard: With _____.
9. Provide aid or assistance.
12. Famous Texas fight: The Battle of the _____.
15. Item not bought by someone; opposite of sold.
17. Des Moines is the capital of this state.
18. Big, elaborate, often formal celebration.
19. Nuclear weapon: _____ bomb.
21. One of the Great Lakes.
22. To make the results of something unfairly favor a particular group: _____ the results.
24. Number represented by Roman numeral X
26. Abbreviation of Northeast.

Independence Day

INDEPENDENCE DAY is celebrated each year by many countries around the world. Costa Rica is one of them. But in what *year* did Costa Rica gain its independence? You can find out in this puzzle.

First, look at the Independence Date Box below. Find each date in the Puzzle Grid. Circle (or highlight) that date. The dates read forward, backward, and diagonally.

Now, look for numbers that are not circled (or highlighted). Read from left to right, top to bottom. Put each number on the lines in the sentence below the grid.

Independence Date Box

Sweden: 1523
United States: 1776
Austria: 1901
Poland: 1918
South Africa: 1931
Israel: 1948
Kenya: 1963

1	1	9	1	8
1	3	0	7	4
8	9	2	7	9
1	1	6	6	1
1	5	2	3	1

Costa Rica gained its independence in ____ ____ ____ ____.

Rebus

Something Costa Rica did away with in 1948.

 E

Write your answer here:

_____

Costa Rica Geography Puzzles

The Countries of Central America

COSTA RICA IS ONE of seven countries in Central America. Do you know the names of the other six? Find out in this puzzle.

First, answer as many of the **Clues** as you can on the next page. Then, look at each letter in the answers. Write that letter in the matching number box in the **Country Grids** below. Work back and forth between the Grid and the Clues until you have the names of the six Central American Countries.

We've done one for you.

Country Grids

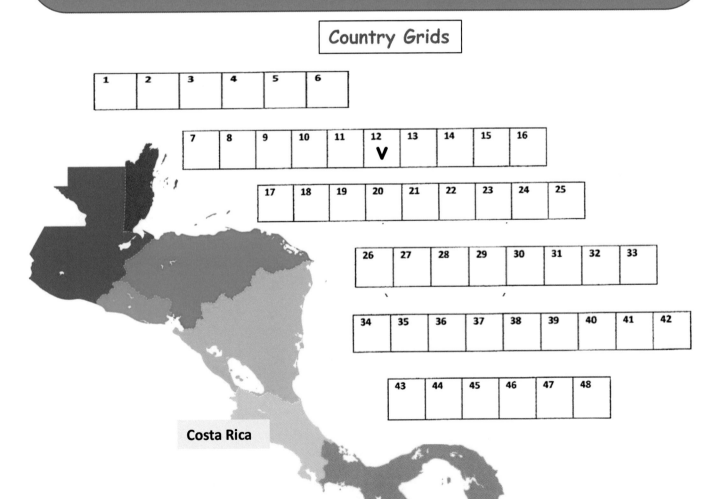

A. Opposite of square. _____ _____ _____ _____ _____
    16   27   18   45   14

B. Bearlike mammal with black rings around its eyes.

    _____ _____ _____ _____ _____
    43   13   28   29   25

C. Something you sit in. _____ _____ _____ _____ _____
    36   26   10   4   38

D. A woolly-haired mammal from South America (related to the camel).

    _____ _____ _____ _____ _____
    3   24   44   22   39

E. Disney character: Mickey _____.   _____ _____ _____ _____ _____
    47   15   30   9   6

F. A very hot flame or light. (Rhymes with gaze.) _____ _____ _____ _____ _____
    1   8   42   5   21

G. A crown of jewels worn on the head by women. _____ _____ _____ _____ _____
    20   35   19   31   32

H. What comes out of an erupting volcano. _____ _____ _____ _____
    11   46   12   37

I. Short for United States of America. _____ _____ _____
    41   33   48

J. Breakfast food. _____ _____ _____
    2   17   40

K. Abbreviation for National Education Association. _____ _____ _____
    34   7   23

Rebus

Where is Costa Rica located?

North America **IN** South America

Write your answer here:

_____

Border Neighbors

ONLY TWO COUNTRIES

border Costa Rica. Panama is to the south. What country borders Costa Rica to the north? Finish this puzzle to find out.

Across

1. Greases.
3. Abbreviation for Georgia.
6. The vocal range between tenor and soprano.
8. American Indian groups.
11. Opposite of down.
12. Used to tell about another choice: "Go out either this door _____ that one."
13. ____ cetera: Latin phrase meaning "*and so forth*" or "*and others.*"
14. **COUNTRY THAT BORDERS COSTA RICA TO THE NORTH.**
19. Opposite of yes.
20. Opposite of off.
21. Stand _____ attention.
22. What a waitress takes.
24. 1950's music: Rock and _____.
26. Short for advertisement.
27. Without cost.

Down

1. Frequently.
2. Something to wear around your neck in Hawaii.
3. Fuel.
4. Short for Albert.
5. Another name for "dad."
7. Short, full skirt worn by ballerinas.
9. Type of snake: _____ constrictor.
10. Mistake.
13. Latin abbreviation meaning "for example."
15. Opposite of "out of."
16. Abbreviation for company.
17. Conjunction: dogs _____ cats.
18. What a bride does at a wedding: *walks down the _____.*
21. Drawings or paintings.
22. Opposite of new.
23. An organ to hear with.
25. Short for Los Angeles.

Population Puzzle

THE POPULATION of Costa Rica is about the same as what U.S. state?

HINT: They each have about 4,800,000 people.

Across

1. Something found in a fireplace; cinder.
4. Internal Revenue Service, for short.
7. City in Brazil: _____ de Janeiro.
8. Also.
9. Short for Los Angeles.
11. "_____ thee I sing."
12. **U.S. STATE WITH SAME POPULATION AS COSTA RICA.**
15. Abbreviation for Pennsylvania.
16. Short for Edward.
17. Opposite of start.
19. A barrier to keep water from flowing freely.
22. The Caspian or Mediterranean _____.
23. Sneaky: "_____ as a fox."

Down

1. Abbreviation for Arkansas.
2. Spanish for yes.
3. Spanish for hello.
4. Pronoun: "Give _____ to me."
5. Place inside a house.
6. Couch.
10. Short for Abraham.
12. Gorillas.
13. A narrow path or alley.
14. Totals; sums.
18. Short for district attorney.
20. Short for Albert.
21. Patriotic song: "_____ Country 'Tis of Thee."

1	2	3		4	5	6
7				8		
		9	10		11	
12	13			14		
15			16			
17		18		19	20	21
22				23		

Quick Fact

Costa Rica has the same land area as which two U.S. states put together. Rearrange the letters to find out.

Y E N   R J W S E E

___ ___ ___   ___ ___ ___ ___ ___ ___

S A T E S H A T C M S U S

___ ___ ___ ___ ___ ___ ___ ___ ___ ___ ___ ___ ___

The Rainforest

LIKE ALL RAINFORESTS, Costa Rica's rainforests are divided into four different levels or layers. Different kinds of plants and animals live in each layer.

You can find the name of each layer in this puzzle. First, answer as many of the **Clues** as you can on the next page. Then, look at each letter in the answers. Write that letter in the matching number in the Rainforest Name Grids below. We've done one for you.

Rainforest Name Grids

				G			
28	29	30	31	32	33	34	35

22	23	24	25	26	27

12	13	14	15	16	17	18	19	20	21

1	2	3	4	5	6	7	8	9	10	11

A. Opposite of finish. ___ ___ ___ ___ ___
                        17   35   23   31   6

B. Sound a cow makes. ___ ___ ___
                       29   2   9

C. Not square. ___ ___ ___ ___ ___
            16   10   12   34   14

D. A mineral; rhymes with more. ___ ___ ___
                       25   3   15

E. A barrier that often separates two houses. ___ ___ ___ ___ ___
                                        1   30   24   22   4

F. Idiom: "Bigger fish to ___." ___ ___ ___
                             7   20   27

G. More than enough. ___ ___ ___ ___ ___ ___
                 26   8   28   13   18   21

H. Injures by stabbing with a horn, antler or tusk

___ ___ ___ ___ ___
    32   19   11   33   5

Did You Know?

COSTA RICA IS KNOWN for its rich, lush, and thick rainforests. The magnificent jungles cover much of the country and are home to more than 500,000 species of plants and animals.

Each year, a tropical rainforest gets up to 260 inches (6,601 mm) of rain. How does that compare to other places in the world? Check out the three boxes below. They show the average rainfall of three cities in the world. Unscramble the letters to find the city and country (or state).

126.7 inches (3,218 mm)	23.4 inches (594 mm)	.3 inches (7 mm)
LOHI, WAHIAI	**DOLNON, DLEGNAN**	**MALI, ERPU**
_____	_____	_____

Who Am I?

I'M ONE OF THE MOST popular "active" volcanoes in Costa Rica. (Scientists say an active volcano is one that could erupt at any time.)

I am located 55 miles (90 km) from San Jose, the capital of Costa Rica.

For 42 years, I erupted many times every day. Red, flowing lava would ooze down my cone-shaped crater. But, then, in 2010, I decided to take a long rest. Maybe by the time you read this, I will have erupted again. Who knows?

So, who am I? To find out, first finish the puzzle on the next page. Then, match the letters in the colored circles to the same colored lines below the puzzle. You will discover my name.

Rebus

What kids like to do at a Costa Rican volcano.

craLOOKter

Write your answer here: _____

Photo: Leonora (Ellie) Enking

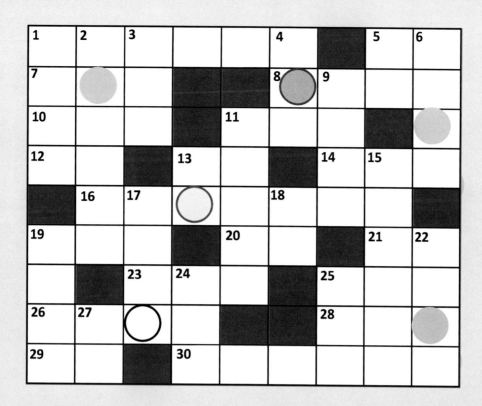

| Blue | Green | Orange | White | Yellow | Pink |

ACROSS

1.   Opposite of dormant or extinct.
5.   Opposite of out.
7.   Short for professional.
8.   Having a score of zero in tennis.
10. What you do at meals.
11. What you do at an auction.
12. Street, abbreviated.
13. Laugh word.
14. What you row a boat with.
16. Things at the end of pencils.
19. Bawl.
20. Short for Edward.
21. Abbreviation for South America.
23. Abdominal muscles, for short.
25. Swine or hog.
26. Opposite of all.
28. To utilize.
29. Emergency room, for short.
30. What an active volcano sometimes does.

DOWN

1.   Gorillas.
2.   A bowl-shaped feature at the top of a volcano.
3.   Child.
4.   _____ Whitney, inventor of cotton gin.
5.   Roman numeral for 4.
6.   Opposite of far.
9.   Smell; scent.
11. Baseball call: "The _____ are loaded."
13. Same as 13 Across
15. Help out; give a hand to.
17. American Idol host, _____ Seacrest.
18. Same as 20 Across.
19. Shape of some volcanos.
22. A long time: "I haven't seen you in _____."
24. An insect that lives in a hive and can sting.
25. Young dog.
27. Either you ____ I will go.

Costa Rican Agriculture

COSTA RICA IS A GREAT PLACE to grow fruits and vegetables. The temperature is warm, the soil is rich, and there's lots of rain.

Today, Costa Rica grows many different kinds of fruits and vegetables, including pineapples, watermelon, and plantains (similar to bananas).

But what was Costa Rica's first agricultural product? Hint: It has been exported (sold to other countries) since the 1790's.

Find out what this product is in this Word Search puzzle. Look at the Word Box. It lists some of the products that Costa Rica grows. Circle or highlight the name of each product in the puzzle grid. Next, write the unused letters on the blanks below. Read from left to right, top to bottom. That will tell you the name of Costa Rica's oldest agricultural product.

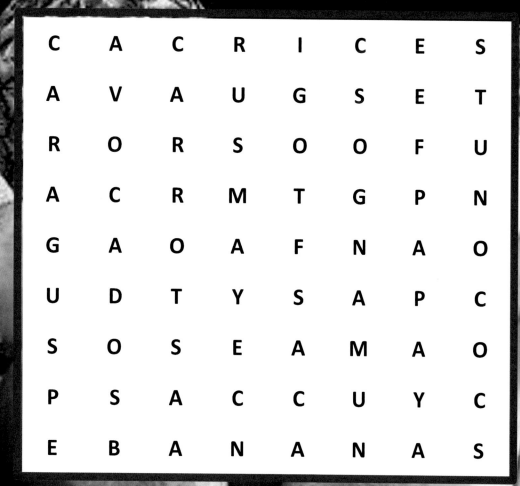

C	A	C	R	I	C	E	S
A	V	A	U	G	S	E	T
R	O	R	S	O	O	F	U
A	C	R	M	T	G	P	N
G	A	O	A	F	N	A	O
U	D	T	Y	S	A	P	C
S	O	S	E	A	M	A	O
P	S	A	C	C	U	Y	C
E	B	A	N	A	N	A	S

Word List

Avocados	bananas	carrots	cas	coconuts
guava	mangos	papaya	potatoes	rice
sugar	yams	yucca		

Visit a Volcano

COSTA RICA HAS MORE than 60 volcanoes. Most are dormant. They haven't erupted in more than 10,000 years.

But six are considered active. Scientists define an active volcano as one that has erupted at least once in the last 10,000 years! The six active volcanos in Costa Rica have erupted at least once in the last four hundred years.

One of those volcanoes is located in Poás Volcano National Park. Poás Volcano is one of the most popular in Costa Rica. It has one of the largest active craters in the world.

See if you can find our way to the Poás Volcano in this puzzle.

Start here!

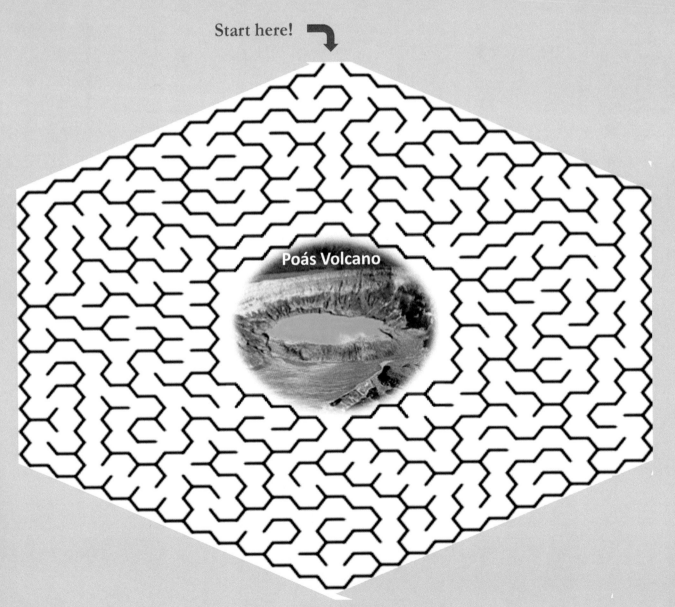

Poás Volcano

Costa Rica People and Culture Puzzles

Welcome to San Jose

IMAGINE you just flew into San Jose, Costa Ria. You land at Juan Santamaria International Airport. You're excited to explore the country.

You head off for San Jose, the capital of Costa Rica. You've heard there is a FABULOUS kids' museum there. It's called the Children's Discovery Museum. You want to check it out. Draw your path from the San Jose International Airport to the Children's Discovery Museum.

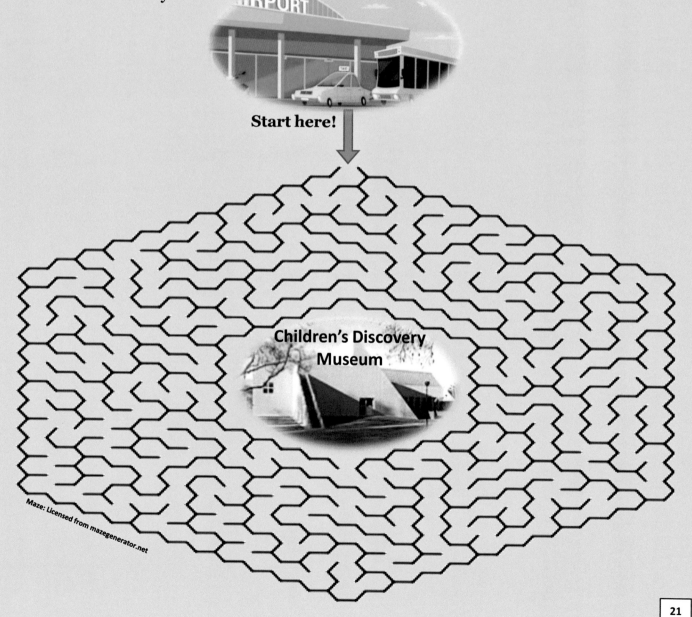

Start here!

Children's Discovery Museum

Maze: Licensed from mazegenerator.net

Picture Puzzle
Juan Santamaria International Airport

Take a look at the two pictures of an international airport below. The two pictures may look the same. But look again. There are ten differences. Can you find the differences between the two pictures? Circle or highlight what you find.

A National Hero

JUAN SANTAMARIA IS THE NAME of Costa Rica's national airport in San Jose. But it is also the name of one of the country's most beloved national heroes -- a young drummer boy in Costa Rica's army who helped win an important battle in 1856.

While in the army, Juan had a special nickname because of his spiked hair. Find out that nickname in this puzzle.

Across

1. Army instruction: "_____ ease."
3. Large deer with large antlers.
7. Corn on the _____.
9. Group of naval ships.
10. The main money used in many countries in Europe.
12. Short for "I have."
13. A territory of the United States: Puerto _____.
15. Roman numeral for 4.
16. **JUAN SANTAMARIA'S NICKNAME.**
19. Short for United Nations.
20. Idiom: "Strong _____ ox." (2 words)
21. City in Brazil: _____ de Janeiro.
23. Same as 3 Across.
25. Opposite of liquid.
27. Short for sister.
29. Opposite of begins.
30. Forward and backward: _____ and fro.

Down

1. Short for air conditioner.
2. What you might stub. "I stubbed my _____ on the chair's leg."
3. Central American country: _____ Salvador.
4. What you might wear around your neck in Hawaii.
5. "Home Alone" movie character: _____ McCallister.
6. Short for Stephen.
8. Something you might say when it's freezing outside.
9. Concentrated on something: "He _____ his attention on the game."
11. Central American country: Costa _____.
14. Gemstone, often used in jewelry.
16. Pocketbook.
17. An herb that can often make you cry when peeled.
18. Fluids used for printing.
22. Opposite of new.
24. Take a seat: "_____ down."
26. Idiom: "The ball _____ in your court."
28. Good-bye: _____ long.

The Name Game

PEOPLE IN COSTA RICA have a special name they call themselves. Finish this puzzle to find out what that name is – for men and for women.

Across

1. An adult, male deer.
5. Abbreviation for United States of America.
8. **NAME FOR A COSTA RICAN WOMAN.**
9. Opposite of closed.
10. Short for Edward.
11. Woman; girl.
13. Stand _____ attention.
14. Encountered; ran into.
16. One type of food.
18. Good-bye in Spanish.
20. To pull along with force. "I had to _____ the bag of cement to the backyard."
21. Pig.
24. Something you say at a wedding: "I _____."
25. Opposite of bottom.
27. Opposite of yes.
28. New or original thought.
30. **NAME FOR A COSTA RICAN MAN.**
32. Short for modern.
33. Word at the end of some prayers.

Down

1. Part of a plant from which leaves and flowers grow.
2. Brand of laundry detergent.
3. Short for air conditioner.
4. Choke.
5. Opposite of down.
6. Sit: "Take your _____."
7. Insect that lives in the ground.
9. Type of butter; margarine.
12. Friend, in Spanish.
15. What a road is often paved with.
17. Cinder.
19. Facts or statistics.
20. An extinct, flightless bird.
22. Opposite of twice.
23. Someone hired to frighten or harm someone else; thug; rhymes with moon.
24. Not bright.
26. Abbreviation for Parent Teacher Association.
29. Gym class: Phys. _____.
31. Contraction for "I am."

"Pura Vida" (POO-rah VEE-dah): It's Everywhere!

IN COSTA RICA, you will hear the term *pura vida* a lot. You might hear it when you ask people how they are. You might hear it when you say hello or good-bye to someone. You might even hear it when someone trips and almost falls.

But what does it mean? Actually, it can mean lots of different things. Finish this puzzle to find one way to define *pura vida*.

Across

1. Talk a lot; chatter.
3. What you might say about someone who is really terrific: "She _____."
7. Opposite of child.
8. Short for laboratory.
10. Abbreviation for Northeast.
11. Consequently; therefore. "It was raining, _____ we couldn't go out to play."
12. A type of shoe, often worn in snow.
14. Covered truck; rhymes with man.
15. **ONE MEANING OF "PURA VITA" (with 16 Across).**
17. Opposite of walk.
18. What a runner in baseball must touch in order to score.
19. On or in the location of: "____ school."
20. Saying: "Sink _____ swim."
21. Short for Irvin.
23. U.S. state known for, among other things, the potato.
24. Opposite of started.
25. Negative word: "No, the boys are _____ here."

Down

1. Opposite of guy.
2. A large, powerful monkey that lives on the ground.
3. The smallest of a litter of dogs or pigs.
4. Expression often heard at a Spanish bullfight.
5. Abbreviation for Connecticut.
6. A small piece of rock.
9. Concerning: "I need a book _____ pyramids."
11. More secure from danger.
13. Overdose, for short.
14. The ability to see: "Her _____ improved with glasses."
15. School question: "What _____ are you in?"
16. Abbreviation for Los Angeles.
18. Actor _____ Pitt.
20. A long, elaborate poem; rhymes with toad.
22. Animal doctor, for short.
23. Short for identification.

The Most Challenging Sports Event On the Planet!

EACH YEAR, Costa Rica hosts what many consider to be the most grueling and challenging sporting event on the planet. Hundreds of competitors come from around the world to take part in the event that lasts four days. Can you guess what it is? Finish this puzzle to find out.

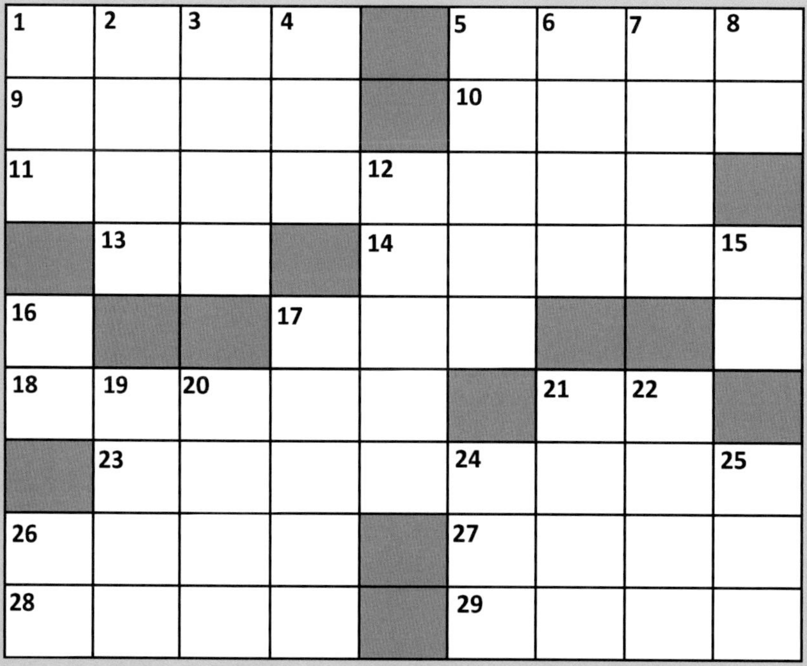

The grid (numbered cells):

Row 1: 1, 2, 3, 4, [black], 5, 6, 7, 8
Row 2: 9, 10
Row 3: 11, 12, [black]
Row 4: [black] 13, [black] 14, 15
Row 5: 16, [black] 17
Row 6: 18, 19, 20, [black] 21, 22, [black]
Row 7: [black] 23, 24, 25
Row 8: 26, 27
Row 9: 28, 29

The Most Challenging Sports Event On the Planet

Across

1. An insect related to the butterfly.
5. Study hard for a test.
9. Musical instrument with long, thin body.
10. Idiom meaning to help: "Give me a _____."
11. **FIRST WORD IN SPORT CHALLENGE.**
13. Emergency room, for short.
14. Puts somewhere so no one can find.
17. 2,000 pounds.
18. Big, formal events; celebration.
21. Something you add sometimes at the end of a letter, abbreviated.
23. **SECOND PART OF SPORT CHALLENGE (2 words).**
26. Different; other: "Give the job to someone_____."
27. Russian ruler in the 1500s: _____ the Terrible.
28. Permits; allows.
29. To change the shape of something to a curve or angle.

Down

1. Opposite of dad.
2. Same as 9 Across.
3. The act of going from place to place to sightsee. "We took a _____ of the rainforest."
4. Opposite of rooster.
5. Circles of metal or other material joined together: _____ -link fence.
6. A sudden, surprise attack; also, product that gets insects to bug off.
7. Novel: _____ *of Green Gables*.
8. Short for medical doctor.
12. Saying: "_____ were the days!"
15. In the same way; also. "He sang well, and _____ did she."
16. Latin abbreviation meaning "for example."
17. Brings along or carries: "He always _____ his umbrella if it looks like rain."
19. Having the skill or opportunity to do something; capable.
20. A series of names or items written one after another.
21. To cover a road with tar or other material.
22. Copy something from a printer into your computer.
24. Bone in the chest.
25. Opposite of start.
26. Country: _____ Salvador.

Cock-a-Doodle-Doo

GALLO PINTO is a favorite dish in Costa Rica. It consists of rice and beans and it is eaten often at breakfast with eggs. But what does "gallo pinto" mean? Find out in this puzzle. Start with the letter **S.** It has a red dot under it. Write the letter S on the first blank in the Answer Grid below. Go clockwise around the wheel. Put every third letter in the next blank. You will discover what Gallo Pinto means.

HINT: It's what you might call a male chicken with measles. LOL!

Answer Grid

____ ____ ____ ____ ____ ____

____ ____ ____ ____

Find the Sodas

IN COSTA RICA, "sodas" are everywhere – not to drink, but for a quick bite to eat. That's because a soda is not a can of Coke or Pepsi, but a small café, like a diner.

See how many "sodas" you can find in this puzzle. The word "soda" runs across, down, diagonally, forward, and backward. Circle (or highlight) each soda. There are 15 of them.

Write the letters that are not circled on the lines below. Rearrange the letters to spell out the name of a popular food you can get at a Costa Rica soda.

A	S	O	D	A	A	L
S	O	D	A	D	O	S
O	D	S	O	D	A	O
D	A	S	O	D	A	D
A	D	O	S	A	D	A
S	O	D	A	M	O	T
S	S	A	D	O	S	E

The unused letters are: ____ ____ ____ ____ ____ ____ ____

I can rearrange those letters to spell ____ ____ ____ ____ ____ ____ ,
a favorite food in Costa Rica.

LOL LOL LOL LOL LOL LOL LOL LOL LOL LOL LOL LOL LOL LOL

A popular beach town in Costa Rica is Jaco (say: ha-co). Change one letter in Jaco to find the name of a Mexican food popular in Jaco.

A favorite food in JACO is a ____ ____ ____ ____ !

Money Talk

WHAT IS THE NAME of Costa Rican money? Finish this puzzle to find out. The answer to all of the clues can be found somewhere in this book.

Clues

A. Favorite sport in Costa Rica. ___ ___ ___ ___ ___ ___ ___

B. National flower of Costa Rica. ___ ___ ___ ___ ___ ___

C. First European in Costa Rica. ___ ___ ___ ___ ___ ___ ___ ___

D. Capital of Costa Rica. ___ ___ ___ ___ ___ ___

E. Country south of Costa Rica. ___ ___ ___ ___ ___ ___

Write the circled letters on the lines below:

___ ___ ___ ___ ___

Rebus

Many people say that Costa Rica is:

MILL1ION

Write your answer here:

_____

People, Places, and Things

DELICIOUS! That's what everyone says about one of the most popular desserts in Costa Rica. It is called *Arroz con Leche*. Do you know what it is? To find out, finish this puzzle.

First, read the Fun Facts about Costa Rica below. Each of the 17 words in bold is hidden in this puzzle. Circle or highlight those words.

Finally, write the unused letters on the lines below the puzzle. Read from left to right, top to bottom.

Claudia Poll

I	R	O	R	C	H	I	D	I	E
N	W	N	C	S	O	D	A	T	Q
S	N	A	K	E	T	E	S	B	U
T	Y	C	T	I	P	E	T	I	A
R	E	L	C	E	R	U	R	R	T
U	K	O	D	O	R	B	O	D	O
M	N	V	F	P	I	F	N	D	R
E	O	I	O	R	S	N	A	C	K
N	M	L	B	A	T	N	U	L	G
T	L	M	U	I	D	A	T	S	L

Franklin R. Chang-Diaz

Answer: Arroz con Leche is:

___ ___ ___ ___ ___ ___ ___ ___ ___ ___

Fun Facts About Costa Rica

1. The national flower is the **orchid.**
2. La Fortuna is a beautiful **waterfall.**
3. The fer-de-lance is the country's deadliest **snake**.
4. The marimba is the national **instrument**.
5. Costa Rica's Franklin R. Chang-Diaz was NASA"s first Latin American **astronaut.**
6. Estadio Nacional is the country's national **stadium**.
7. Deep fried plantains are a favorite **snack**.
8. A small, family-style restaurant is called a **soda**.
9. Irazú is the country's highest **volcano.**
10. Costa Rica is located about 888 miles (1,429 km) north of the **equator.**
11. A Costa Rican man is called a **tico.**
12. The white-faced capuchin **monkey** is one of four species of monkeys in Costa Rica.
13. The **Bribri** people lived in Costa Rica long before Columbus arrived.
14. The Monteverde Cloud **Forest** is home to the quetzal, the most colorful **bird** in the country.
15. As of 2018, Claudia **Poll** is the country's only Olympic gold medalist.
16. About 110 of the 1,100 **bat** species in the world live in Costa Rica.

31

Fun Facts about Costa Rica

WANT TO DISCOVER some fun facts about Costa Rica? There are five fun facts in this puzzle. To find out what those fun facts are, just follow the directions on the next page.

1 200	5 the	2 the	1 of	4 anthem	2 the
3 41	5 the	4 national	5 exporter	1 reptiles.	3 the
2 capital	4 every	5 pineapples	3 than	1 different	2 world.
5 in	3 of	4 morning	5 largest	4 the	5 world.
4 7:00	5 of	3 50	2 humingbird	4 a.m.	2 of
3 states.	4 at	3 smaller	4 plays	1 species	3 U.S.

1. Write all of the Number 1 words or numbers here.

_____

Now rearrange those words to finish this sentence.

Costa Rica has_____

2. Write all of the Number 2 words here.

_____

Now rearrange those words to finish this sentence.

Costa Rica is_____

3. Write all of the Number 3 words or numbers here.

_____

Now rearrange those words to finish this sentence.

Every Costa Rican radio station _____

4. Write all of the Number 4 words here.

_____

Now rearrange those words to finish this sentence.

Costa Rica _____

5. Write all of the Number 5 words here.

_____

Now rearrange those words to finish this sentence.

Costa Rica is_____

Picture Puzzle
Costa Rican Soccer

THE MOST POPULAR SPORT in Costa Rica is soccer (or, as Costa Ricans call it, fûtbol). In almost every town in the country, you will find a soccer field.

In fact, Costa Rica ranks number 1 in the world as far as the percentage of the total population that plays soccer. In the United States, fewer than 8 percent of the population plays soccer; in England, fewer than 7 percent; and in Australia, fewer than 5 percent. In Costa Rica, nearly 27 percent of the population plays soccer!

Take a look at the two pictures of the Costa Rica soccer player below. The two pictures may look the same. But look again. There are ten differences. Can you find the differences? Circle or highlight what you find.

Costa Rica Wildlife Puzzles

A Visit to Manuel Antonio National Park

COSTA RICA'S RAINFORESTS are some of the most beautiful and biodiverse rainforests in the world. One of the most popular, though smallest, is Manuel Antonio National Park. You're sure to see monkeys, sloths, and lots of birds.

See if you can find your way to Manuel Antonio in this puzzle.

Start Here

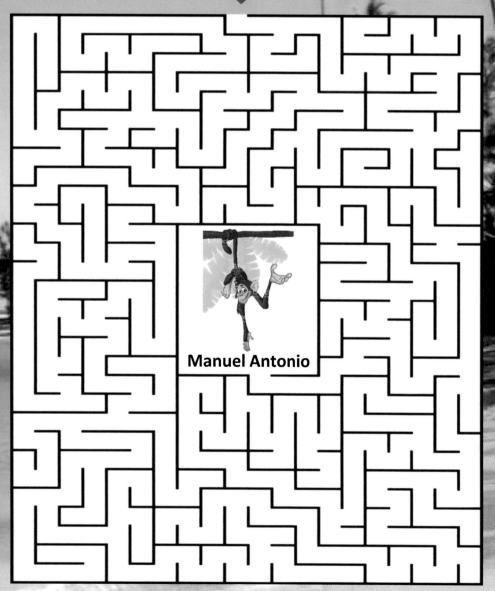

Manuel Antonio

Maze: Licensed from mazegenerator.net

Who Am I?

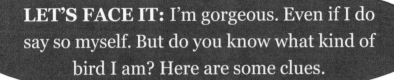

LET'S FACE IT: I'm gorgeous. Even if I do say so myself. But do you know what kind of bird I am? Here are some clues.

I'm a member of the parrot family.

I'm about 32 inches (81 cm) long. Half of that is my tail.

I weigh about 2.2 pounds (1 kg).

I'm known to make very loud sounds.

In Costa Rica, I'm only found on the Pacific Ocean side of the country.

So who am I?

To find out, look at the circle. Some letters of the alphabet are missing. Write those letters on the lines below.

Now, rearrange those letters to spell out my name. (You can use letters more than once.) I put the letter A in the right spaces for you.

The missing letters are:

_____ _____ _____ _____ _____ _____ _____ _____

I can rearrange those letters to spell.

_____ _____ __A__ _____ _____ _____ _____

_____ __A__ _____ __A__ _____

y o z j u h p
g y n v d i
f x
b q k

36

The Howling Howler

THE HOWLER MONKEY is one of four species of monkeys in Costa Rica. There is something special about this monkey. What is that? To find out, first cross out all the words in the grid:

- that can be read the same forward and backward
- that are pronouns
- that rhyme with sing
- that name a color
- that are compound words
- that are misspelled
- that mean the "same as" small
- that mean the "opposite of" small

Now read the words that are not crossed out from top to bottom, left to right. **Write what's special about the Howler Monkey here.**

_____

wow	sting	It's	neice	I	notebook
cowboy	green	large	you	the	little
libery	loudest	red	madam	he	tiny
thing	ninty	wing	big	animal	freind
they	recieve	doghouse	on	toot	its
black	noon	blue	we	downtown	Earth

Rebus

A favorite bird in Costa Rica.

2 [can image]

Write your answer here: _____

Guess the Name

CAN YOU GUESS what the name is of this cute, little guy? Find out by finishing this puzzle.

Look at the Word Box. It lists the names of some of the other animals in Costa Rica.

Circle or highlight each one in the puzzle grid.

Now write the unused letters on the blanks below the puzzle. Read from left to right, top to bottom. They spell out the name of this Costa Rican animal.

BTW, if you want to see this cute guy, look in the trees. He hardly ever comes down to the forest floor.

Word Box
Anteater, Armadillo, Bats, Heron, Jaguar, Macaw, Monkey, Ocelot, Sloth, Tapir, Toucan, Turtle, Viper.

R	T	O	U	C	A	N	E	J
A	D	B	E	T	R	V	Y	A
N	W	A	C	A	M	I	E	G
T	M	T	D	P	A	P	T	U
E	O	S	T	I	D	E	U	A
A	N	L	R	R	I	R	R	R
T	K	E	E	S	L	O	T	H
E	E	E	F	C	L	R	L	O
R	Y	H	E	R	O	N	E	G

___ ___ ___ - ___ ___ ___ ___ ___

___ ___ ___ ___ ___ ___ ___ ___ ___

Hidden Monkey

COSTA RICA has four species (or types) of zany, crazy, playful monkeys – all of them fun to watch.

One of the species is hiding in this puzzle. Can you find its name?

First, read about this special monkey in the box below. Each **bold** word in the text is hidden in the puzzle grid. Find and circle (or highlight) each word.

Now write the unused letters on the lines below. Read from top to bottom, left to right.

TIP: Circle the words in the text as you find them in the puzzle.

B	S	T	A	D	U	L	T
A	S	S	A	P	I	I	R
R	Y	E	G	D	E	A	E
K	P	R	I	M	A	T	E
I	O	O	L	C	I	R	T
N	N	F	E	U	E	M	O
G	A	T	R	O	O	P	P
O	C	F	N	K	E	Y	S

The monkey hiding in this puzzle is the

_____ _____ _____ _____ _____ ____

_____ _____ _____ _____ _____ ____

The **primate** hidden in this puzzle is one of four **species** of monkeys in Costa Rica. This **agile** monkey almost always stays high off the ground in the **canopy** of the rain **forest**.

He likes to soar through the **treetops** using his long forelimbs and very long **tail** to hold on to branches.

A **troop** of these monkeys usually consists of an **adult** male, a few adult females, and their children. They often warn others of danger by **barking**, But they also "talk" by whining and screaming.

These monkeys are almost exclusively *frugivores*. That means they eat mostly **fruit.**

Sadly, this species and the other three monkeys of Costa Rica are all considered endangered.

Swinging Like a Monkey

HAVE YOU EVER WONDERED what it would be like to swing from tree to tree across the top of a rainforest? You can find out in Costa Rica in one of the many "tours" in rainforests throughout the country.

But what is this special tour called? Find out in this puzzle.

Across

1. Short for Thomas.
3. Having the skill or power to do something: "Birds are _____ to fly."
7. Something you might say if you hit your thumb with a hammer.
9. Fairy tale: "The _____ Piper."
10. Respects; looks up to; has a high opinion of.
13. Opposite of from.
14. Saying: "_____ be it!"
15. Fewer than two.
17. **SPECIAL RAINFOREST TOUR.**
20. Past tense of lead.
21. And so forth (Latin). _____ cetera.
22. Shakespeare play: "_____ You Like It."
24. Opposite of Western.
27. Crosses over: Bridges often _____ rivers.
29. Opposite of off.
30. Another word for quiz or exam.
31. Short for debutante or Deborah.

Down

1. This and _____.
2. Opposite of dad.
3. Large mammal, such as a gorilla or chimpanzee.
4. Large North American mammal that some say looks like a buffalo.
5. Famous book for kids and adults: _____ Petit Prince (The Little Prince)
6. Idiom meaning excited or nervous: "On the _____ of my seat."
8. Small bit of something: "A _____ of hair."
11. Sleep lightly; nap.
12. Parts in a play.
16. Opposite of far.
18. Thoughts or pictures formed in the mind: "She has some great _____ for the party."
19. What you might say when you want something: "Give ____ ____ me." (2 words.
20. Opposite of first.
23. A stuck-up person; rhymes with rob.
25. Small insect, often red or black.
26. Opposite of start.
28. Short for physical education.

1		2			3	4	5	6
		7	8		9			
10	11			12				
13			14			15	16	
	17	18			19			
20				21			22	23
		24	25			26		
27	28				29			
30					31			

Rebus

People often say that the squirrel monkeys are:

Funny Funny

Words Words Words Words

Write your answer here:

_____

Costa Rica's National Bird

IF YOU LOVE BIRDS, then Costa Rica is the place to visit. It has more than 900 different species (or kinds) birds. The bird pictured here is Costa Rica's national bird. Do you know what it's called? Find out in this puzzle.

First, look at the Word Box. It has the name of 10 Costa Rican birds. Circle or highlight each one in the puzzle grid. Some appear more than once. The number next to each name tells how many times it appears in the puzzle.

H	Q	T	T	R	O	G	O	N	C	H
M	U	O	M	A	N	A	K	I	N	U
A	E	M	L	A	A	Y	L	K	O	M
G	T	T	M	C	C	A	O	A	G	M
P	Z	O	L	I	Z	A	O	N	O	I
I	A	M	R	T	N	E	W	A	R	N
E	L	D	E	A	W	G	T	M	T	G
J	H	U	C	B	A	R	B	E	T	B
A	Q	U	M	A	C	A	W	I	R	I
Y	O	T	A	N	A	G	E	R	R	R
T	U	M	O	T	M	O	T	S	H	D

Word Box

Hummingbird (2)	Trogon (2)
Quetzal (2)	Manakin (2)
Magpie Jay (1)	Barbet (1)
Toucan (1)	Macaw (3)
Motmot (2)	Tanager (1)

Now, look for all the letters that are not highlighted. Read from left to right, top to bottom. Write each letter on the lines below.

The name of the national bird of Costa Rica is the

___ ___ ___ ___-___ ___ ___ ___ ___ ___ ___

___ ___ ___ ___ ___ ___

Puma Roundup

THE PUMA IS ONE of six species of wildcat in Costa Rica. It is the second largest after the jaguar.

How many pumas can you find in this puzzle? Start with the letter P with the red dot. Go clockwise around the wheel. Use each letter only once. How many times did you count the word "puma"?

Answer: I found _____ pumas in this puzzle.

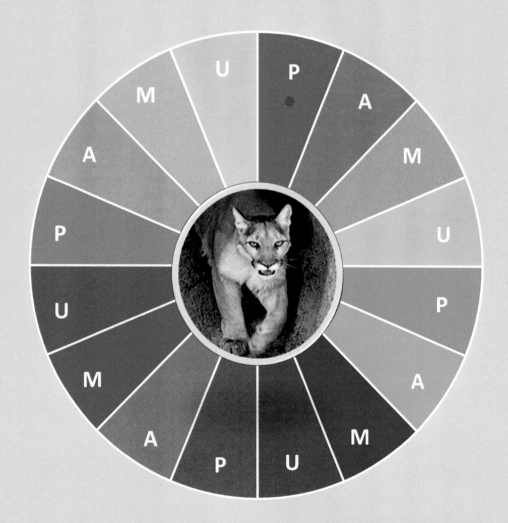

Quick Take

Can you turn the word PUMA into something you might see on a fancy bird.

● Add one new letter ● Change one vowel to a different vowel.

What word do you have? _____

Play Date

LOOK AT THE FOUR popular Costa Rican animals above. They include the squirrel monkey, the toucan, the sloth, and the hummingbird.

In this puzzle, there are seven groups of these four animals. Can you find those seven groups?

Here's some help. The groups run across, down, or diagonally. The four animals are not in any order. No animal in a group intersects or crosses with another group. Circle or highlight the seven different groups of these four animals.

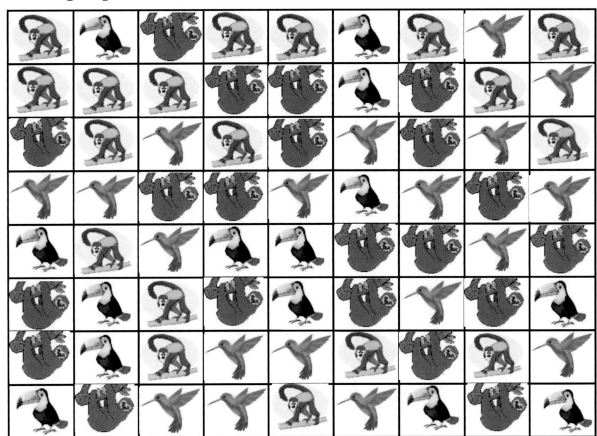

Rebus

The two best times to hear the very loud (almost scary) sound of the howler monkey.

BBBB dawn

Noon Late

Write your answer here:_____

Monkey Business

COSTA RICA IS KNOWN for its four fun-to-watch monkeys. One of them is the frantic white-faced Capuchin monkey pictured here. You can find the names of the other three in this puzzle.

Start with the red letters S in the wheel.

It has the blue dot under it. Write the letter S on the first blank on the lines below. Go clockwise around the wheel. Put every third letter in the next blank. You will discover the names of Costa Rica's three other monkeys.

— — — — — — — — — — — —

— — — — — — — — —

— — — — — — — —

Picture Puzzle: The Costa Rican Jungle

THE RAINFORESTS OF COSTA RICA are home to more than 500,000 species of plants, insects, and wildlife.

Take a look at the two pictures of some of the wildlife in a typical rainforest. The two pictures may look the same. But look again. There are ten differences. Can you find the differences between the two pictures? Circle or highlight what you find.

The Wildcats of Costa Rica

COSTA RICA IS HOME to six different species (or kinds) of wildcats. Find out the names of the six cats in this puzzle. How?

Match the letters in the Puzzle Code box to the same letter/number in the Wildcat boxes. For example, D3 in the Puzzle Code box stands for the letter "O." Put the letter "O" on each line below labeled D3.

Puzzle Code	1	2	3	4
A	N	L	R	G
B	C	P	T	D
C	J	E	Y	A
D	M	I	O	U

Its Spanish nick- name is mano gordo (or fat hand). These "fat hands" help this cat climb trees quickly.

___ ___ ___ ___ ___ ___
D3   B1   C2   A2   D3   B3

This cat, which is about the size of a house cat, can imitate sounds of its prey in order to catch it easier.

___ ___ ___ ___ ___ ___
D1   C4   A3   A4   C4   C3

This is Costa Rica's Big Cat. It can grow to over 6 feet (2 m) in length and weigh up to 250 pounds (113 kg).

___ ___ ___ ___ ___ ___
C1   C4   A4   D4   C4   A3

This is the second largest of the Costa Rica cats and is one of only two cats that doesn't have a spotted coat.

___ ___ ___ ___
B2   D4   D1   C4

This shy cat is the smallest of Costa Rica's six cats. It lives mainly high in the mountains

___ ___ ___ ___ ___ ___ ___
D3   A1   B1   D2   A2   A2   C4

This relative of the jaguar looks more like a weasel than a wildcat. It is the only cat that is active primarily during the day.

___ ___ ___ ___ ___ ___ ___ ___ ___
C1   C4   A4   D4   C4   A3   D4   A1   B4   D2

Adventure Riddle

What do you call a sightseeing tour by air?

To find out, finish this puzzle. First, look at the Word Box. It has words that tell about fun things to do in Costa Rica.

Circle or highlight each word in the puzzle. Then, write the unused letters on the lines below the puzzle. Read from top to bottom, left to right. You will discover the answer to the riddle.

C	R	U	I	S	E	L
S	A	I	L	F	E	E	L
I	R	M	G	P	H	K
H	S	A	P	T	S	A
S	U	A	F	S	I	Y
W	R	E	E	T	F	A
I	F	I	W	A	L	K
M	N	B	I	K	E	G

Word Box

BIKE
CAMP
CRUISE
FISH
KAYAK
RAFT
RAPPEL
SAIL
SURF
SWIM
WALK

A sightseeing tour by air is called

___ ___ ___ ___ ___ ___ ___ ___ ___ ___ ___ ___

Visit a Surfer's Paradise

COSTA RICA HAS SOME OF THE BEST BEACHES IN THE WORLD. In fact, there are more than 300 beaches along more than 800 miles (1,287 km) of coastline along the Pacific Ocean and Caribbean Sea.

Some people say the best beach for kids is on the Caribbean side of the country. It's called Punta Uva. Draw your path from San Jose to Punta Uva.

Start here!

Punta Uva

Maze: Licensed from mazegenerator.net

3 Fun Things for Kids to Do in Costa Rica (Parents, too!)

WANT SOME IDEAS for some fun things to do in Costa Rica? Here are three.

First, answer as many of the **Clues** as you can on the next page. Then, look at each letter in the answers. Write that letter in the matching number blank in the Things to Do Grids below. Work back and forth between the Grid and the Clues until you discover three fun things for kids to do in Costa Rica (and their parents, too!)

We've done one for you

Things to Do

1

___ ___ ___ ___ ___ ___ ___ ___ ___ ___ ___
1   2   3   4   5   6   7   8   9   10 11

2

___ ___ ___ ___ ___ ___ ___ ___ ___
12 13   14 15   16 17 18 19   20

___ ___ _L_ ___ ___ ___ ___
21   22 23   24   25 26 27

3

___ ___ ___ ___ ___ ___ ___ ___
28 29   30 31   32   33 34 35

___ ___ ___ ___ ___ ___ ___
36 37   38 39   40   41 42

Fun Things to Do Clues

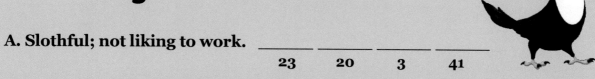

A. Slothful; not liking to work. ___ ___ ___ ___
                                              23   20   3   41

B. Idiom: ___ **tag: what people play when they keep leaving messages for each other.**

___ ___ ___ ___ ___
5   32   2   17   14

C. One of a pair, often identical. ___ ___ ___ ___
                                             18   28   7   26

D. What cowboys use to lasso cattle. ___ ___ ___ ___
                                             15   22   12   40

E. Opposite of floor. ___ ___ ___ ___ ___ ___ ___
                  31   13   4   6   9   38   11

F. The earth's natural satellite. ___ ___ ___ ___
                                      36   19   27   8

G. Money. ___ ___ ___ ___
          24   29   42   34

H. Idiom: "Like ___ **candy from a baby."** ___ ___ ___ ___ ___ ___
                                        33   25   39   16   10   1

I. What you do in an election. ___ ___ ___ ___
                              21   37   30   35

Rebus

What you do when you go snorkeling.

$$\frac{\text{WATER}}{\text{EXPLORE}}$$

Write your answer here:

_____

What Am I?

A POULAR PLACE TO VISIT in Costa Rica is Tortuguero National Park. In fact, it's the third most visited park in the country, even though you can only get to it by boat or plane. Why is it so popular?

One reason is to see the nesting site of an amazing group of reptiles.

Each year from February to July, these reptiles come ashore, dig their nest in the sand, and lay their eggs. It's an awesome thing to watch!

What kind of reptile is it? Find out in this puzzle.

Start with the red letter **L** with the blue dot under it. Write that letter on the first blank on the lines below. Go clockwise around the wheel. Put every third letter in the next blank. You will discover the name of this awesome reptile. TIP: Cross out the letters in the wheel as you use them.

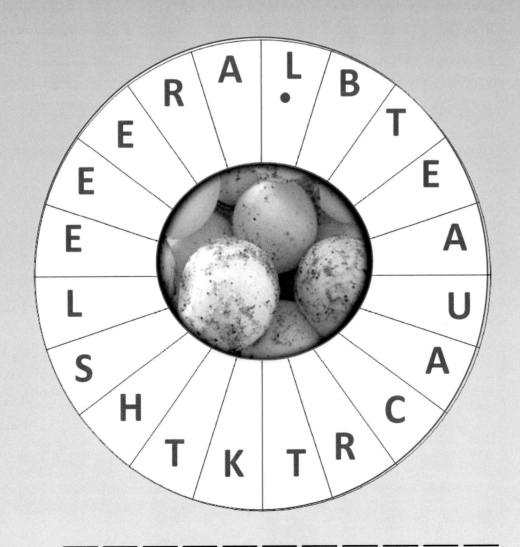

__ __ __ __ __ __ __ __

__ __ __ __ __ __

Puzzle Answers

Page 5: What Columbus Named CR

A	D	S			L	E	S	
C	U	T	S	A	R	K		
T	O	O	T		T	E	A	M
		R		B	E		T	O
T	H	E	G	A	R	D	E	N
H	E		A	T		R		
E	A	R	S		S	E	T	S
	T	O	E		T	A	I	L
	S	I	S			M	A	Y

Page 6: What Does It Mean

L	O	L			A	M		
A	R	I	D		C	O	A	T
	E	L		F		O	L	E
		A	T	O	P		P	S
R	I	C	H	C	O	A	S	T
A	N		E	A	T	S		
I	T	S		L		H	A	
N	O	U	N		G	E	R	M
		M	E			S	E	E

Page 8: Costa Rican Holiday

L	E	S			T	A	P	E
O	A	T	H		I	D	E	A
S	C	R	E	A	M		A	S
S	H	E	L	L		U	S	E
		S	P	A	I	N		
G	A	S		M	O	S	E	S
A	T		T	O	W	O	R	K
L	O	N	E		A	L	I	E
A	M	E	N			D	E	W

Page 12: Border Neighbors

O	I	L	S		G	A		P
F		E			A	L	T	O
T	R	I	B	E	S		U	P
E			O	R		E	T	
N	I	C	A	R	A	G	U	A
	N	O		O	N			I
A	T		O	R	D	E	R	S
R	O	L	L			A	L	L
T		A	D		F	R	E	E

Page 13: Population Puzzle

A	S	H			I	R	S
R	I	O		T	O	O	
		L	A		O	F	
A	L	A	B	A	M	A	
P	A		E	D			
E	N	D		D	A	M	
S	E	A			S	L	Y

Page 17: Who Am I

A	C	T	I	V	E		I	N
P	R	O			L	O	V	E
E	A	T		B	I	D		A
S	T		H	A		O	A	R
	E	R	A	S	E	R	S	
C	R	Y		E	D		S	A
O		A	B	S		P	I	G
N	O	N	E			U	S	E
E	R		E	R	U	P	T	S

A	R	E	N	A	L
Blue	Green	Orange	White	Yellow	Purple

53

Puzzle Answers, cont.

Page 23: A National Hero

A	T				E	L	K	S
C	O	B		F	L	E	E	T
	E	U	R	O		I	V	E
		R	I	C	O		I	V
P	O	R	C	U	P	I	N	E
U	N		A	S	A	N		
R	I	O		E	L	K	S	
S	O	L	I	D		S	I	S
E	N	D	S				T	O

Page 24: The Name Game

S	T	A	G			U	S	A
T	I	C	A		O	P	E	N
E	D		G	A	L		A	T
M	E	T		M	E	A	T	
		A	D	I	O	S		
	D	R	A	G		H	O	G
D	O		T	O	P		N	O
I	D	E	A		T	I	C	O
M	O	D			A	M	E	N

Page 25: Pura Vida

G	A	B		R	O	C	K	S
A		A	D	U	L	T		T
L	A	B		N	E		S	O
	B	O	O	T		V	A	N
G	O	O	D		L	I	F	E
R	U	N		B	A	S	E	
A	T		O	R		I	R	V
D		I	D	A	H	O		E
E	N	D	E	D		N	O	T

Page 27: Sports Challenge

M	O	T	H		C	R	A	M
O	B	O	E		H	A	N	D
M	O	U	N	T	A	I	N	
	E	R		H	I	D	E	S
E			T	O	N			O
G	A	L	A	S		P	S	
	B	I	K	E	R	A	C	E
E	L	S	E		I	V	A	N
L	E	T	S		B	E	N	D

Page 41: Swinging Like a Monkey

T	O	M			A	B	L	E
H		O	W		P	I	E	D
A	D	M	I	R	E	S		G
T	O		S	O	O	N	E	
	Z	I	P	L	I	N	E	
L	E	D		E	T		A	S
A		E	A	S	T	E	R	N
S	P	A	N		O	N		O
T	E	S	T				D	E	B

Page 9: Independence Day

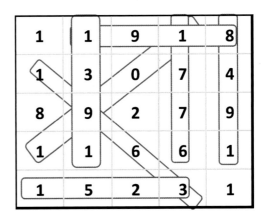

1	1	9	1	8
1	3	0	7	4
8	9	2	7	9
1	1	6	6	1
1	5	2	3	1

54

Page 19: Agriculture

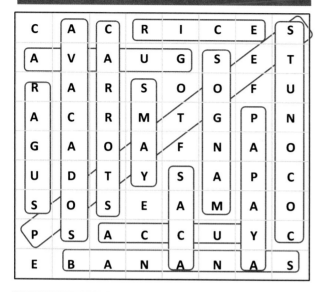

Page 29: Find the Soda

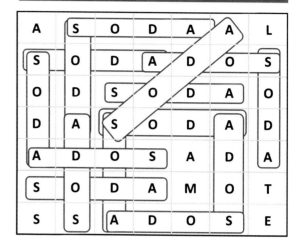

Page 39: Hidden Monkey

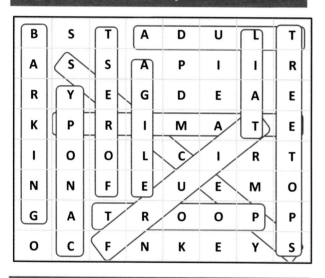

Page 38: Guess the Name

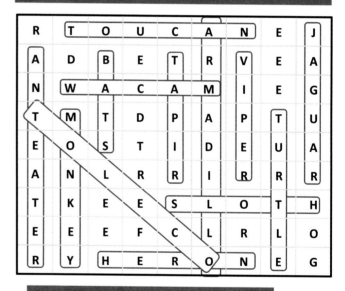

Page 42: Costa Rica's National Bird

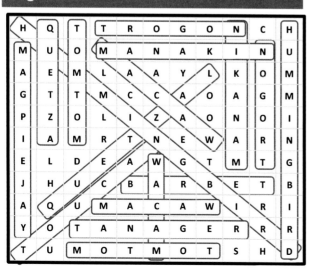

Page 48: Adventure Riddle

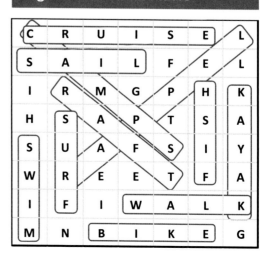

Puzzle Answers, cont.

Page 31: People, Places, and Things

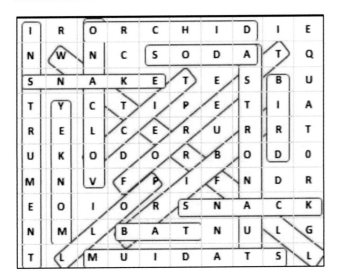

Page 10: Countries of Central America

Answers

1. Belize; 2 El Salvador; 3. Guatemala; 4. Honduras; 5. Nicaragua; 6. Panama

A. **Opposite of square: ROUND**
B. **Bearlike mammal with black rings around its eyes: PANDA**
C. **Something you sit in: CHAIR**
D. **A woolly-haired mammal from South America): LLAMA**
E. **Small rodent: MOUSE**
F. **A very hot flame or light. BLAZE**
G. **A crown of jewels worn on the head by women: TIARA**
H. **What comes out of an erupting volcano: LAVA**
I. **Short for United States of America. USA**
J. **To hire, employ or retain the services of someone: ENGAGE**

Page 14: Rainforest

Answers

The layers of the rainforest are (top to bottom): Emergent, Canopy, Understory, Forest Floor

A. Opposite of finish: START
B. Sound a cow makes: MOO
C. Not square: ROUND
D. Opposite of less: MORE

E. A barrier that often separates two houses: **FENCE**
F. Idiom: Bigger fish to: **TO FRY**
G. More than enough: **PLENTY**
H. Injures by stabbing with a horn, antler or tusk: **GORES**

Page 47: The Wildcats of Costa Rica

Answers
OCELOT
MARGAY
JAGUAR
PUMA
ONCILLA
JAGUARUNDI

Page 44: Play Date

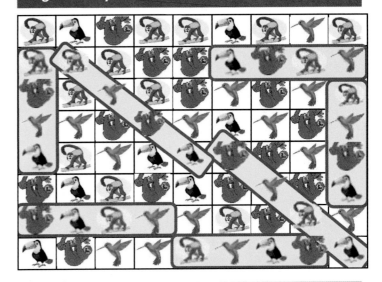

Page 50: 3 Fun Things to Do

Answers
1. Go ziplining
2. Peer into a volcano
3. Watch the monkeys

A. Slothful: **LAZY**
B. What people play when they keep leaving messages for each other: **PHONE** tag
C. One of a pair, often identical: **TWIN**
D. What cowboys use to lasso cattle: **ROPE**
E. Opposite of floor: **CEILING**
F. What shines at night: **MOON**
G. Money: **CASH**
H. Idiom: "Like _____ candy from a baby": **TAKING**
I. What you do in an election: **VOTE**

Page 4: Columbus Discovers CR

Page 20: Visit a Volcano

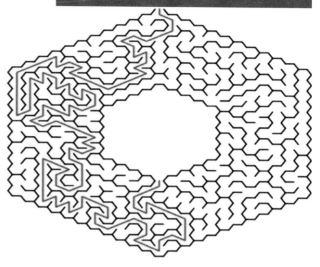

Page 21: Let's Visit San Jose

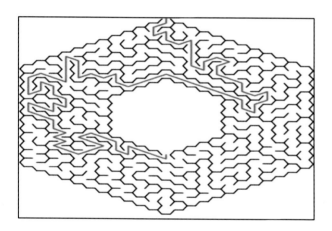

Page 35: A Visit to Manuel Antonio

Page 49: A Surfer's Paradise

Miscellaneous

Page 7: Electricity
Page 13: Massachusetts and New Jersey
Page 15: Hilo, Hawaii, London, England, Lima, Peru
Page 29: Taco
Page 43: Plume

Puzzle Answers, cont.

Page 7: Coat of Arms Picture Puzzle

The differences are (from top down):
1. The knot in the ribbon is green.
2. One of the seven stars is missing.
3. One sun ray is missing.
4. The green land area under the volcanoes is larger.
5. The flag on the back of the ship is missing.
6. There is a missing yellow dot on the far left of the shield.
7. There are only three circles on the bottom of the shield.
8. An orange spot at the bottom of the far right volcano is missing.
9. Curley cue on upper left
10. Line in the green leaf on right is missing.

Page 34: Soccer Picture Puzzle

The differences are (from top to bottom):
1. The top of the flag pole is missing.
2. A wisp of hair on the back of the boy's head is missing.
3. There is an extra curl over the forehead of the boy.
4. The boy's right shirt sleeve is longer.
5. The boy's shirt collar is different.
6. A line in the soccer ball is missing.
7. There is only one stripe on the boy's pants.
8. The boy's sock on his left leg is not turned down.
9. There is an extra shoe lace in the boy's right sneaker.
10. The bottom of the flag pole is shorter.

Page 22: Airport Picture Puzzle

The differences are (from top to bottom):
1. The line in the "O" of Airport is missing.
2. One line in the curve of the roof is missing (far right).
3. The airplane in the sky on the right is missing.
4. A small sign within a sign over the entrance doors to the airport is missing.
5. The destination sign on the bus is missing.
6. One of the rearview mirrors on the scooter is missing.
7. One red caution light on the front of the taxi is missing.
8. The rear door handle on the taxi is missing.
9. The rearview mirror on the far side of the bus is missing.
10. The rear tire of the bus is missing.

Page 46: Jungle Picture Puzzle

The differences are (form top to bottom):
1. The hummingbird at the top of the picture is missing.
2. One spot on the anaconda snake is missing.
3. There is an extra butterfly to the left of the parrot.
4. The tail of the blue parrot on the far left is shorter.
5. The small tree in center by river is missing.
6. The trunk of the tree on the left splits up higher.
7. The frog in the middle, bottom of the picture is missing.
8. The vine that is creeping up the side of the tree on the right is shorter.
9. The river is much narrower at one point than in the original.
10. The leaf at the bottom, middle of the picture has no veins in it.

Miscellaneous

Page 28: Cock-A-Doodle Doo
Answer: Spotted Rooster

Page 30: Money Talk
Answer: Colón

Page 32-33: Fun Facts
Answers
1. **Costa Rica has** 200 different species of reptiles.
2. **Costa Rica is** the humming-bird capital of the world.
3. **Costa Rica is** smaller than 41 of the 50 U.S. states.
4. **Every Costa Rican radio station** plays the national anthem every morning at 7:00 a.m.
5. **Costa Rica is** the largest exporter of pineapples in the world.

Page 36: Who Am I?
Answer: Scarlet Macaw

Page 37: The Howling Monkey
Answer: It's the loudest animal on earth.

Page 43: Puma Roundup
Answer: 4 pumas in the puzzle wheel
Answer: Plume

Page 52: Who Am I?
Answer: Leatherback Sea Turtle

Rebuses

Answers
Page 4: 4 Different Tribes
Page 7: Army
Page 10 In between North America and South America
Page 16: Look inside a crater
Page 29: One in a million
Page 35: Toucan
Page: 40 Too funny for words
Page 42 Before dawn and late afternoon
Page 48: Explore underwater

To Our Valued Customers

Curious Kids Press is passionate about creating fun-to-read books about countries and cultures around the world for young readers, and we work hard every day to create quality products.

All of our books are Print on Demand books. As a result, on rare occasions, you may find minor printing errors. If you feel you have not received a quality printed product, please send us a description and photo of the printing error along with your name and address and we will have a new copy sent to you free of charge. Contact us at: info@curiouskidspress.com

Thank you.

Curious Kids Press

42227065R00038

Made in the USA
Lexington, KY
14 June 2019